THE FIRST WITH THE LATEST!

Aggie Underwood,
the *Los Angeles Herald*,
and the Sordid Crimes of a City

Joan Renner
Edited by Christina Rice

photo
friends

LOS ANGELES PUBLIC LIBRARY

This catalog was published in conjunction with a photo exhibit at
Los Angeles Central Library's History & Genealogy Department—
The First with the Latest!
Aggie Underwood, the *Los Angeles Herald*,
and the Sordid Crimes of a City
August 3, 2015–January 13, 2016

Thank You! Kim Creighton, Terri Grant, Wendy Horowitz, Michelle Olivier, and Fernando Saucedo.

The First with the Latest!
Aggie Underwood, the *Los Angeles Herald,* and the Sordid Crimes of a City
Written by Joan Renner • Edited by Christina Rice
Copyright © 2015 Joan Renner
Images Copyright © 2015 Los Angeles Herald Examiner Collection/Los Angeles Public Library

Published by:
Photo Friends of the Los Angeles Public Library
c/o Future Studio
P.O. Box 292000
Los Angeles, CA 90029

www.photofriends.org

Designed by Amy Inouye, Future Studio Los Angeles

Special quantity discounts available when purchased in bulk by corporations, organizations, or groups. Please contact Photo Friends at: **photofriendsla@gmail.com**

ISBN-13: 978-0692703458

Printed in the United States

photo
friends
LOS ANGELES PUBLIC LIBRARY

*Dedicated to
Agness "Aggie" Underwood,
Newspaperwoman*

CONTENTS

Opposite: Aggie hard at work in the 1960s

THE FIRST WITH THE LATEST!

Aggie Underwood, the *Los Angeles Herald*, and the Sordid Crimes of a City

A gness "Aggie" Underwood never intended to become a reporter—all she really wanted was a pair of silk stockings. She'd been wearing her sister's hand-me-downs, but she longed for a new pair of her own. When her husband told her they couldn't afford them, she threatened to get a job and buy them herself. It was an empty threat. She had no idea how to find employment. It was pure serendipity when a close friend phoned the day after the stockings kerfuffle and told her that there was a temporary opening for a switchboard operator at the *Los Angeles Record*. The job was meant to last only through the 1926-1927 holiday season so Aggie jumped at the chance.

Aggie arrived at the *Record* knowing nothing about the newspaper business, but she was a quick study and it was apparent to everyone that, although untrained, she was bright and eager to learn. The temporary switchboard job turned into a permanent position.

In December 1927 the city was horrified by the kidnapping and cruel mutilation murder of twelve-year-old schoolgirl Marion Parker. Aggie was at the *Record* when they received word that the perpetrator, William Edward Hickman, who had nicknamed himself "The Fox," had been captured in Oregon. The breaking story created a fire storm of activity in the newsroom—Aggie had never seen anything like it. She realized then that she didn't want to be a bystander. She wanted to be a reporter.

When the *Record* was sold in January 1935, Aggie made the leap into the big leagues by accepting an offer from William Randolph Hearst's newspaper the *Evening Herald and Express*. Working for Hearst was completely different than working for the *Record*. Hearst's reporters were expected to work at breakneck speed, after all they had to live up to the paper's motto, "the first with the latest."

From January 1935 until January 1947 Aggie covered everything from fires and floods to murder and mayhem, and frequently with photographer Perry Fowler by her side. She was considered a general assignment reporter but developed a reputation for covering crimes.

Sometimes, she helped solve them.

In December 1939 Aggie was called to the scene of what appeared to be a tragic accident on the Angelus Crest Highway. Laurel Crawford said that he had taken his family on a scenic drive, but lost control of the family sedan on a sharp curve. The car plunged over 1000 feet down an embankment killing his wife, three children, and a boarder in their home. He said he had survived by jumping from the car at the last moment.

When asked by Sheriff's investigators for her opinion, Aggie said she had observed Laurel's clothing and his demeanor and neither lent credibility to his account. She concluded that Laurel was "guilty as hell." Her hunch was right. Upon investigation, police discovered that Laurel had engineered the accident to collect over $30,000 in life insurance.

Hollywood was Aggie's beat too. When stars misbehaved or perished under mysterious or tragic circumstances, Aggie was there to record everything for *Herald* readers. On December 16, 1935, popular actress and café owner, Thelma Todd, died of carbon monoxide poisoning in the garage of her Pacific Palisades home. Thelma's autopsy was the first Aggie ever attended. By the time it was over all of Aggie's colleagues had turned green and fled the room—only she and the coroner's staff remained upright.

Though Aggie never considered herself a feminist, she certainly paved the way for female journalists. When she was suddenly yanked off the notorious Black Dahlia murder case in 1947 and made the editor of the City Desk, she was the first woman to hold this post for a major metropolitan newspaper. Known to keep a bat and startup pistol handy at her desk, just in case, she was beloved by her staff and served as City Editor for the *Herald* (later *Herald Examiner*) until retiring in 1968.

When she passed away in 1984, the *Herald Examiner* eulogized her by printing, "She was undeterred by the grisliest of crime scenes and had a knack for getting details that eluded other reporters. As editor, she knew the names and telephone numbers of numerous celebrities, in addition to all the bars her reporters frequented. She cultivated the day's best sources, ranging from gangsters and prostitutes to movie stars and government officials."

Through the Los Angeles *Herald Examiner's* photo archive, now held by the Los Angeles Public Library, the cases Aggie covered are more than just faded headlines, but come to life in light and shadow. As you can see, her notebook was filled with some of the most Deranged L.A. Crimes ever perpetrated in Los Angeles, and Aggie sometimes served as more than just an observer.

Joan Renner
Author/Editrix/Publisher of *Deranged L.A. Crimes*
(derangedlacrimes.com),
Board Member of Photo Friends

On November 7, 1956, Agness Underwood was the featured guest on the popular television show *This is Your Life,* hosted by Ralph Edwards. Here, Aggie is shown with Edwards (*left*) and David Hearst, publisher of the Los Angeles *Herald* where Aggie served as a long-time reporter and editor.

This is a
TepLo-Phone Booth
PATENTED
MADE BY THE TEPLO PHONE BOOTH CO.
LOS ANGELES

Aggie at her desk in 1949, two years after becoming the city editor for the Los Angeles *Herald and Express*. She kept a baseball bat handy in case she needed to keep overzealous Hollywood press agents in line.

Opposite: Aggie horsing around for Perry Fowler's camera in an oddly shaped telephone booth.

Aggie takes a break at a local watering hole.

Opposite: Aggie and some staff at the Los Angeles *Herald* celebrate her tenth anniversary as city editor in 1957.

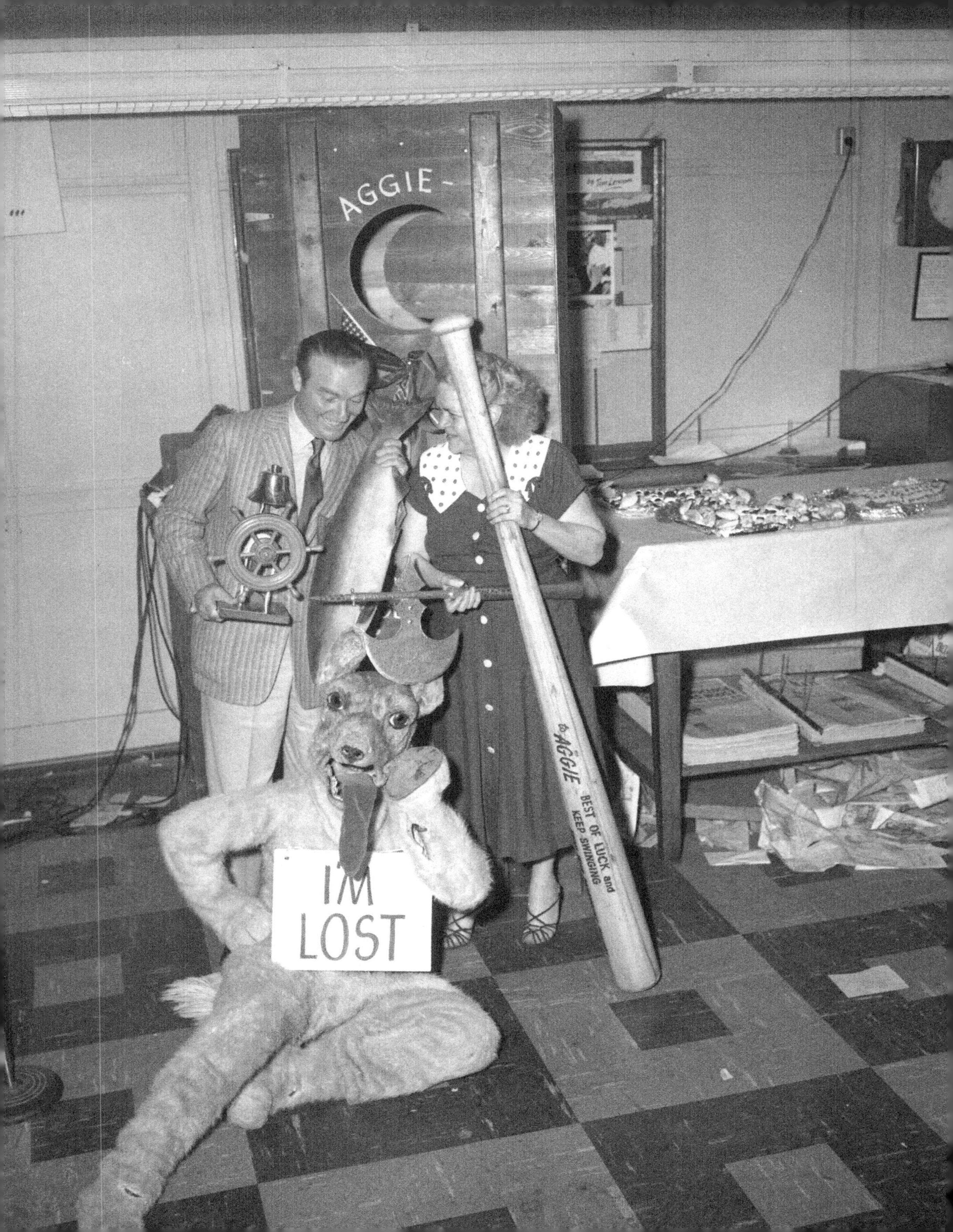
AGGIE -
I'M
LOST
to AGGIE BEST OF LUCK and
KEEP SWINGING

Aggie takes a swing at *Herald* staffer with a rubber fish while celebrating her tenth anniversary as city editor at the newspaper.

The First with the Latest!

Aggie, and a host of other local reporters gather around actress Jayne Mansfield as she prepares to board a DC-7C for its inaugural flight to Mexico City for Mexicana-Pan American Airways.

Aggies celebrates her birthday with *Herald* staffers in 1960.

Opposite: Aggie gets into the holiday spirit at a *Herald* staff party in December 1957.

Aggie in 1960, revisiting her humble beginnings as a switchboard operator.

Opposite: Aggie receives a proclamation naming her "Newspaperwoman of the Year, 1961" from Council Member Harold Henry (*left*) and Mayor Sam Yorty.

The First with the Latest!

Aggies sits opposite Phoebe Hearst, whose twin brother, George Randolph Hearst Jr. was the publisher of the Los Angeles *Herald*.

Opposite: Aggie speaks before the Greater Los Angeles Press Club in 1961.

WILLIAM EDWARD HICKMAN

On December 15, 1927, twelve-year-old schoolgirl Marion Parker was unwittingly handed over to a monster by the school registrar at Mt. Vernon Junior High School. Her abductor had come to the school that day and said that Perry Parker, the girl's father, had been seriously injured in an automobile accident and was calling for his *youngest* daughter, but Marion was a twin—which girl had he meant? Marion happened to be the easiest to reach that day and so it was she who went with the man.

Two days after Marion's kidnapping, Perry received a telegram reiterating an earlier demand for $1,500 in exchange for his daughter's life. That evening Parker took a call from the kidnapper. The man instructed him to drive to the corner of Fifth Street and Manhattan Place and told him not to inform the cops or the girl would die. Parker was to sit in his car and wait for the kidnapper to pull up next to him to show him that Marion was alive. The kidnapper would then collect the ransom money and drop Marion off a block down the street.

Parker followed the kidnapper's instructions to the letter. He waited at the designated meeting place for a few minutes before a Chrysler coupe pulled up beside him. He looked over and caught a glimpse of Marion sitting in the front seat. Parker sensed that something was wrong—maybe she was bound or drugged. Nothing could have prepared him for the reality.

The driver of the Chrysler had a white handkerchief over his face and

Opposite: **Hickman being locked up by Chief Jailer Frank Dewar, left, and Deputy Ray Bogie, on December 27, 1927.**

The apartment house at 1170 Bellevue Avenue where William Edward Hickman is asserted to have lived. A blood-stained towel monogrammed "Bellevue Arms Apartments" was found at the kidnapping drop site. Police found Hickman in the apartment that night but decided not to arrest him until a reward would be offered two days later. Meanwhile he escaped and was found by police in Oregon. Marion Parker was believed to have been killed in this building

The First with the Latest!

pointed a large caliber weapon at Parker. He said: "You know what I'm here for. Here's your child. She's asleep. Give me the money and follow instructions." The money was exchanged and Parker followed the coupe down the block. The passenger door of the car opened and Marion was pushed out onto a lawn.

The Chrysler roared off and Parker ran over to Marion. He felt a few moments of relief. But when Parker got to Marion and took her in his arms he saw that not only was she dead but she had been savagely mutilated, eyelids sewn wide open, and her limbs hacked off. His screams made an unholy sound that reverberated throughout the neighborhood.

Marion's killer was identified as William Edward Hickman, a former employee at Parker's bank. Aggie Underwood was in the newsroom at the *Record* when the law caught up with him in Oregon. He was returned to Los Angeles where he was tried and convicted of first degree murder. The firestorm of activity around the Hickman case inspired Aggie to become a reporter.

Hickman died on the gallows in San Quentin on October 19, 1928.

Opposite: Detective D.W. Longuevan, left, talking with Pilot R. M. Lloyd just before taking off from Clover field on December 11, 1927, to fly to Sacramento and on to Salem, Oregon, for William Edward Hickman.

The First with the Latest!

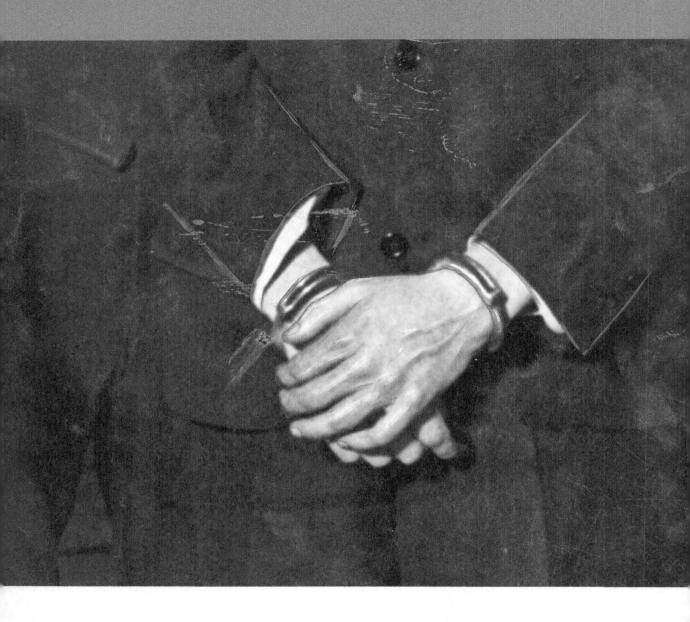

Close up of accused killer William Edward Hickman's cuffed hands. Hickman was the subject of the largest manhunt in Los Angeles history for the gruesome mutilation murder of twelve-year-old schoolgirl, Marion Parker. Aggie Underwood was in the *Daily Record* newsroom when the wire crackled with word that the killer had been captured. At that moment Aggie knew she wanted to be a reporter.

The First with the Latest!

A crowd gathered on the street in front of the Hall of Justice, during the trial of William Edward Hickman.

William Edward Hickman

BURMAH AND THOMAS WHITE

In August of 1933, nineteen-year-old Burmah, a hairdresser and former Santa Ana High School student, and her husband of less than one week, twenty-eight-year-old Thomas White, an ex-con, spent their honeymoon on a crime spree. The couple perpetrated ten stick-ups—seven in a single evening; but the worst of their crimes was the shooting of a popular elementary school teacher, Cora Withington, and a former publisher, Crombie Allen.

Crombie was teaching Cora how to drive his new car. They were stopped at a light when a car driven by a young blonde woman pulled up alongside them, and a man brandishing a gun jumped out of the vehicle. The bandit pointed his weapon at Cora's head and said: "Shell out, sweetheart..." Just as Cora and Crombie were handing over their valuables there was a gunshot— and it tore through Miss Withington's left eye, came out near the right eye and ripped a hole in Allen's neck. Despite his injury, Allen memorized the license plate number of the bandit's car. Both victims survived their wounds, but Cora was permanently blinded.

The cops located the Whites' car in a parking lot adjacent to an apartment on S. Coronado Street. An officer dressed in a mechanic's uniform staked out the vehicle and watched as Burmah got into it and drove it into a garage while her husband held the door open for her. Two officers entered the hallway of the apartment and confronted Thomas, who made the mistake of attempting

Opposite: The *Herald* photographers shot pretty, blonde Burmah White extensively and she seemed to love the attention.

Pictured is a reenactment of the hold-up at Occidental and Third where Crombie Allen and Cora Withington were shot by Thomas and Burmah White.

The First with the Latest!

to shoot it out rather than surrender. He took two bullets to the heart. During the melee, Burmah attempted to either commit suicide or escape by hurling herself out of a window. Police grabbed her before she could jump and took her to jail.

Burmah's lack of remorse and abrasive demeanor were great fodder for the press, but earned the young widow a guilty conviction on eleven felony counts, and she was sentenced to a term of from 30 years to life. She began serving her time at San Quentin, but was ultimately transferred to the Women's Prison at Tehachapi where, in 1935, Aggie Underwood interviewed her and a few of the other inmates for a multi-part series on women in prison. Aggie noted that her attitude had completely changed and Burmah even wrote an open letter to young women entitled "Crime Never Pays."

Burmah was denied parole a few times before she was discharged on December 1, 1941. She'd served less than eight years for her part in the 1933 crime spree. Upon her release, Burmah vanished from public view.

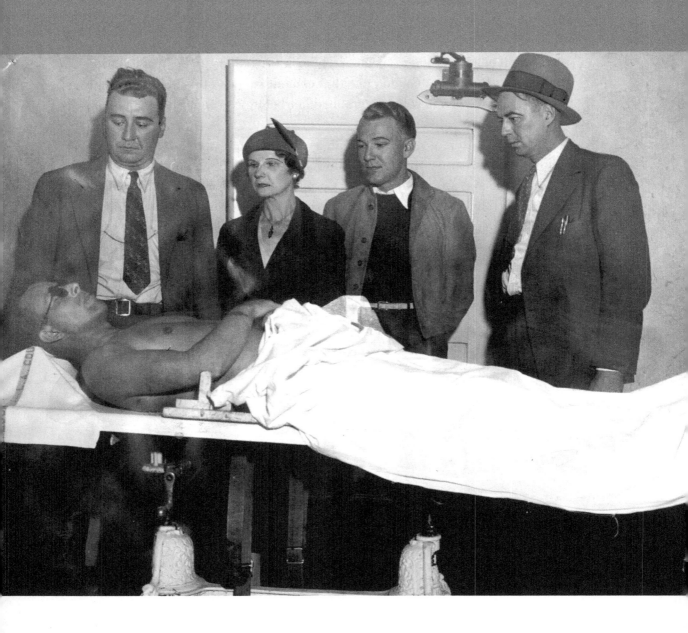

Thomas White (morgue table) was felled by a volley of police bullets as he sought to evade arrest. Flanked by detectives, two of his victims identify him as the man who robbed them at gunpoint. He and his wife Burmah spent their honeymoon on a violent crime spree. If you are wondering why the dead man is wearing sunglasses, they were probably put on his face by a bored morgue attendant with a wicked sense of humor.

The First with the Latest!

Burmah White views the bullet-ridden body of Thomas White, her husband of five days. With her are attorney Donald Mackay (*left*) and Detective Lieutenant Leroy Sanderson. The *Herald* noted that, "She haughtily walked into the morgue and posed with icy indifference, then like an actress going into a 'sob scene' she managed to sniffle a bit."

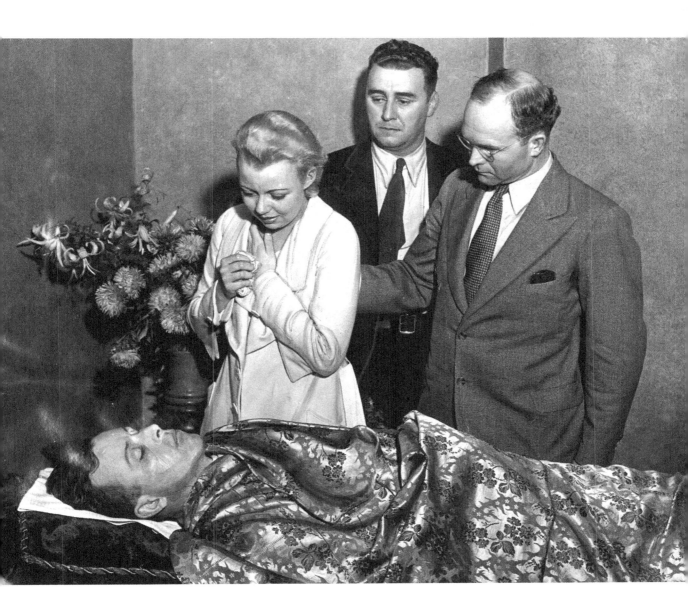

Burmah and Thomas White

Former students of Cora Withington make contributions to the "Cora B. Withington Fund" that was established to help the teacher with mounting expenses cause by being shot and blinded by Thomas and Burmah White.

Opposite: Burmah White (*standing*) was a hairdresser in Santa Ana before she married Thomas and embarked on a short but bloody life of crime. The 19 year-old is smiling in the photo but during her trial she was surly and unrepentant. Aggie Underwood interviewed Burmah two years later at Tehachapi prison and her attitude had completely changed. She wrote an open letter to young women entitled "Crime Never Pays."

The First with the Latest!

NELLIE MADISON

Nellie Madison was a rebel from the time she was a little girl. She was married for the first time in 1908 at age thirteen to a man eleven years her senior. Her parents had the marriage annulled but that didn't slow her down. By 1934, she was on her fifth marriage.

Spouse number five was Eric Madison, an abusive schemer. He proposed to Nellie as soon as he discovered that she had inherited $1,000. He was unable to hold on to a job and he was unfaithful. Nellie came home one day and found him in bed with a sixteen-year-old girl. Eric wasn't contrite, he mocked her and confessed that he had only married her for her money and then he beat her. His rage continued for nearly a week. Nellie was so afraid for her life that she bought a gun.

On March 24, 1934, Eric and Nellie were arguing. It was about midnight and Eric was in bed and Nellie was standing at its foot. She pulled out her gun, but Eric continued to curse at her and from underneath the bed he pulled out a box of butcher knives. He threw a couple of them at Nellie. When he turned to reach for another one, Nellie shot him five times in the back, and then she ran.

She was found two days later and indicted for Eric's murder. District Attorney Buron Fitts vowed to seek the death penalty.

Historically, women who refuse to conform to the norms of society pay a price, and Nellie was a life-long non-conformist. During the trial her

Opposite: Accused murderess Nellie Madison during her trial.

Nellie Madison testifies during her trial for the murder of her husband, Eric. She was convicted and sentenced to hang, though the sentence would be commuted to life in prison.

multiple marriages, childlessness, and unconventional life style weighed heavily against her; perhaps even more than the evidence. The public and the jurors were confounded by the fact that she never dissolved into tears or begged for mercy. The newspapers called her "Sphinx Woman" and "Iron Woman." No one was surprised when she was sentenced to death by hanging.

Her life was spared in 1935 by California's governor, Frank Merriam, after a long and very public sympathy campaign in which Aggie Underwood played a pivotal role. Aggie publicized the case and revealed that Nellie had suffered terrible abuse at Eric's hands. It was not until 1942 that Nellie's life sentence was commuted to a sentence of fifteen years, making her eligible for parole.

Upon her release from Tehachapi, she thanked Aggie profusely saying: "You did it! You did it! I owe it all to you!"

Opposite: Nellie Madison stands stone-faced in prison after being convicted in June 1934 of murdering her husband, Eric Madison. The first degree murder verdict doomed her to death on the gallows.

Portrait of Eric Madison, husband of Nellie who died at her hands after inflicting continuous abuse on her.

Opposite: Nellie Madison is shown in the gardens of the Tehachapi women's prison in September 1935, shortly after having her death sentence commuted to life in prison. She would have been the first woman executed in California, but Aggie Underwood wrote articles that challenged the outcome of the trial. Aggie's articles and public outcry convinced the governor to commute Nellie's sentence to life in prison.

CLARA PHILLIPS

In early July 1922, Clara Phillips visited the hardware department of a local five and dime store; she picked up a fifteen-cent hammer and weighed it in her hand for a moment before turning to the clerk to ask: "Do you think that this is heavy enough to kill a woman with?" The clerk, thinking that this was a joke, replied: "Yes it is, if you hit her hard enough with it." Clara bought the hammer.

The day after she'd purchased the suitable-for-slaying hammer, Clara, a former chorus girl and film extra, spent the afternoon in a Long Beach speakeasy with her friend, another ex-chorine, Peggy Caffee. Clara told Peggy about the back-fence gossip she'd heard that hinted at an affair between her husband Armour and an attractive widow, Alberta Meadows. By the end of the day Clara had formulated a plan to eliminate her rival.

Fabricating a story of needing a lift, Clara and Peggy caught a ride with an unsuspecting Alberta. On a secluded stretch of Montecito Drive, Clara asked Alberta to pull over for a private conversation; she then brought the fifteen-cent hammer down on Alberta's head and battered her until the weapon broke. For the coup de grace Clara rolled a 50-pound boulder onto her victim's chest. Peggy had witnessed the horrific crime from the car, and not wanting to end up like Alberta, she took Clara's advice and kept her mouth shut.

Opposite: **This photo shows the interior of Mrs. Philipps' cell and an opening made by cutting three bars. The theory was that she sawed them, aided by Jesse Carson. But he declared, 'She didn't saw any bars. I just drove up, she walked out with a man and got into my car.'**

This photo-diagram of the old county jail shows the two versions of Clara Phillips' escape following her conviction in the murder of Alberta Meadows. Officers said she crawled out her cell window (*large arrow point*), slid down a drain pipe to the adjoining roof and reached street by the route indicated by dotted line. Jesse Carson, who helped her, said she walked right out the main jail door, shown by right arrow.

The First with the Latest!

Clara Phillips

Clara fled town but she was busted in Tucson and returned to Los Angeles. She was dubbed "Tiger Girl" for the brutality of her attack on Alberta. Clara was tried and found guilty of second degree murder.

On December 5, 1922, it was reported that Clara had escaped from the county jail by cutting the bars of her cell, hoisting herself on to the roof of the building, and then shimmying down a drain pipe. She was on the lam for over four months before she was discovered hiding out in Tegucigalpa, Honduras. The fugitive was arrested and extradited to California, where she began serving her sentence in San Quentin.

Clara was released from Tehachapi in June 1935 after serving twelve years of a life sentence, and Aggie Underwood was there to get an interview. When Clara was asked

Profile view of Peggy Caffee, a key witness in the case against her friend Clara Phillips, who brutally attacked and killed Alberta Meadows.

about her husband, Armour, the man for whom she committed murder, she said: "Really, I don't want to speak of him."

Opposite: **Chief of Detectives Herman Cline examines a garment believed to have belonged to murder victim Alberta Meadows.**

Clara Phillips is accompanied by sheriffs William Traeger (*left*) and Gene Biscailuz at Le Grande Station in Los Angeles and greeted by throngs of reporters following her extradition from Honduras for the hammer murder of Alberta Meadows—a rival for her husband's affections. Her escape from the Hall of Justice Jail and her flight to Central America made headlines for weeks.

The First with the Latest!

Clara Phillips (*center*) served 12 years in prison for the 1922 brutal hammer slaying of Alberta Meadows. Aggie Underwood (*right foreground*) was at Tehachapi for the killer's release on June 17, 1935. Her piece on Clara's return to the world made the front page. Clara left prison with a fanfare, but then slipped quietly into obscurity as a dental assistant in San Diego.

ROBERT "RATTLESNAKE" JAMES

Alabama native Major Raymond Lisenba, *aka* Robert James, moved to Los Angeles during the 1920s. By April of 1935 he owned a barber/beauty shop in downtown Los Angeles. Despite the Great Depression, business was so good that he advertised for a manicurist to add to his growing staff. An attractive blonde, Mary Bush, applied for the position and not only did she get the job, within a couple of months she had married the boss.

On August 4, 1935, Robert and two friends, Viola Lucek and Jim Pemberton pulled up to the La Cañada–Flintridge bungalow he shared with Mary. They were surprised to find the place dark. After calling Mary's name and getting no reply, they began to search for her. They found her slumped forward over the edge of the backyard fish pond. She was unresponsive and appeared to have drowned.

The coroner ruled Mary's death a tragic accident, but while interviewing James, Aggie Underwood found his bored yawns suspect for a man whose wife had just died. She voiced her suspicions to the authorities, and subsequent events proved that Mary's husband had indeed murdered her in a particularly heinous way.

Robert made a rookie mistake when he concocted the plot to kill his wife—he used an accomplice. Accomplices are the weak link in any criminal

Opposite: **Robert James (*right*), barber shop Casanova, and a Deputy identified as George Perdue, en route to the courtroom for James' murder trial. James was charged with murdering his fifth and last bride, who was found half submerged in the fishpond of their La Cañada home. It was discovered that before Mrs. James was drowned, James tried to poison her with deadly rattlesnakes.**

Investigators gather around the fish pond at the rear of the La Cañada home of Robert S. James where his wife, Mary Busch, was found dead of an apparent drowning.

Opposite: These two large Colorado diamondback snakes used in the murder and that appeared in court—Lethal and Lightning allegedly were used by Robert James and Charles Hope to poison James' wife, Mary Busch, were displayed during the murder trial.

The First with the Latest!

enterprise. Robert's accomplice, Charles Hope, had a minor conscience and a major drinking problem. He unburdened himself to a barroom companion, and it resulted in an investigation into Mary's death. The police had never felt completely comfortable with the coroner's ruling that Mary's death was accidental, but even they could not have imagined the details of the real story.

Robert had promised Charles a cut of the life insurance he'd taken out on Mary. Charles was instructed to purchase rattlesnakes. He found two, named Lethal and Lightning, at a snake farm in Pasadena. With Mary blindfolded and tied to the kitchen table, Robert took a box containing the snakes and plunged Mary's foot into it. The snakes struck repeatedly. But Mary didn't die fast enough to suit her impatient husband—he finally ended her agony by drowning her in the bathtub, then staging the fish pond scene.

Police suspected that Robert had murdered one of his previous wives and may have been responsible for the death of a nephew, but they were never able to prove the cases.

The depth and breadth of Robert's depravity may never be known, but he paid the ultimate price for Mary's slaying. He was the last man to be legally hanged in California.

Opposite: The *Herald* summed up the mood of this photo perfectly by writing, "Out from behind the iron bars of his jail cell, Robert James, cigar-smoking, wise-cracking barber shop Casanova, was to come to court here today to hear himself sentenced to hang till he is dead on the gallows at San Quentin. James, shown nonchalantly smoking a cigar in jail while doom hangs over his head, was convicted of the rattlesnake torture and drowning of his bride. The jury's failure to recommend mercy makes it mandatory for the court to sentence him to die."

The First with the Latest!

Murder accomplice Charles Hope shown shortly after collapsing on the stand during the Robert James murder trial. "James' eyes drive me crazy. I could feel him trying to hypnotize me, but I kept talking," he proclaimed while testifying. Later on, Hope would write Aggie Underwood letters from San Quentin.

The First with the Latest!

In May 1936, nine months after her death, Mary Busch's body was exhumed to investigate the accusation that her husband, Robert James, poisoned her with rattlesnakes before drowning her. When her body was checked in the morgue, doctors announced they found on her toe a mark apparently made by the fang of a rattlesnake, which checked out with the strange story told by accomplice Charles Hope, who charged that James held his wife's foot in a box of deadly rattlesnakes.

Robert "Rattlesnake" James

LEROY DRAKE

In September 1935, the bodies of Henry and Nellie Steinheur were dragged out of the water at the end of Pier 146 in Wilmington. They had been reported missing by their nineteen-year-old nephew, Leroy Drake. He first told the police that he feared they had entered into a suicide pact. Under questioning, he revised his story. He said that he had come home to find the pair dead, and it appeared to him that they had been poisoned. Because he had recently been busted on an auto theft charge, he had hesitated to report the incident, and instead he'd driven the bodies out to the pier and dumped them into the water.

The police weren't buying Leroy's tale for a minute, but the kid didn't seem much like a killer. He was an honor student at Long Beach City College, and planned to matriculate at California Institute of Technology. Why would someone with such a brilliant future commit a double murder? When he finally copped to the crime, he said he'd only killed them to spare them the pain and humiliation of having to deal with his arrest for auto theft. Was he lying?

To get to the truth, detectives conducted a reenactment of the slayings. For some reason reliving the night of the murders loosened Leroy's tongue. Maybe it was the sight of the coffee percolator in which he had poured the lethal poison. As he walked around the home with the police he alternately sobbed and then laughed hysterically. In any case, he finally felt compelled

Opposite: Leroy Drake plays the violin for a *Herald* photographer in the home where he had murdered his aunt and uncle with cold calculation the previous day.

to reveal the actual motive. A few weeks before the murders, Leroy learned that Henry had made a will and made him its beneficiary. He would inherit one-third of the estate, *unless* Nellie predeceased him—in that case Leroy would get everything.

After being charged, Aggie and *Herald* photographer Perry Fowler visited Drake in his cell. Perry couldn't believe his ears when he heard Aggie say to Leroy, "...you poor thing. Now suppose you tell me all about it." It was part of her technique to get the suspect talking, and it worked perfectly. Aggie got her story.

On December 12, 1935, Leroy pleaded guilty to two counts of murder in Superior Judge Vickers' court. It was the only way he could be sure he wouldn't die on the gallows. He expressed no regret for what he had done, in fact he said: "I believe I was right. I had to do it, I had to kill them. They were suffering horribly because I had stolen an automobile. I thought I was going to prison for stealing the car, and I knew if that happened, they couldn't live."

Leroy insisted that feeding them poisoned coffee was the merciful thing to do. "I loved them too dearly to let them suffer. But other people don't look at this thing the way I do."

Judge Vickers definitely had a different perspective on the murders than Leroy had, and he sentenced the young man to life in prison. Leroy spent only 21 years in San Quentin before being paroled on July 18, 1957.

Opposite: **Leroy Drake exchanges smiles with sweetheart Vula Hayden who had been called as a witness by the prosecution. Drake went to Miss Hayden's home and calmly discussed violin music moments after having killed the aunt and uncle who reared him.**

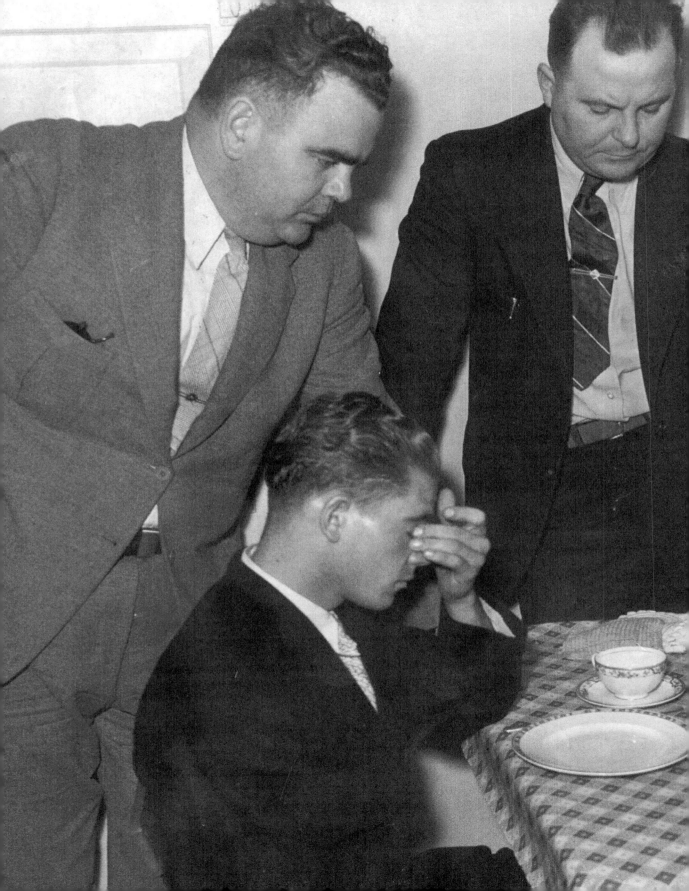

On September 26, 1935, nineteen-year-old Leroy Drake served poisoned coffee to his aunt and uncle and then went to the movies with a girlfriend. When he returned from his night out Leroy placed the bodies in his uncle's car and sent it off a dock into Los Angeles Harbor. Here, he reenacts the "death table" scene for the authorities.

Leroy Drake stands calmly with Public Defender Ellery Cuff as he is sentenced to life in prison for murdering his caretakers.

Opposite: Leroy Drake cooling his heels in a cell after being charged with the poison murders of his aunt and uncle. This photo was taken by Aggie Underwood's colleague and friend, Perry Fowler. Perry couldn't believe his ears when he heard Aggie say to Leroy, "…you poor thing. Now suppose you tell me all about it." It was part of her technique to get the suspect talking, and it worked perfectly.

Leroy Drake

HAZEL GLAB

Much of Hazel Belford Glab's past was, as they say, shrouded in mystery. However, the bits that are part of the public record are very interesting. Hazel had been in trouble with the law numerous times in her both her home state of Oklahoma and in California. Her infractions had been minor—small scale cons and such—until June 19, 1928, when she became the prime suspect in the shooting death of her husband, John I. Glab.

John had been ambushed in the street behind the San Fernando Valley home he shared with Hazel. Hazel tried to sell the murder as a possible mob hit. John was a retired pharmacist from Chicago, and Hazel intimated that he was a bootlegging pal of gangster Al Capone. It wasn't completely out of the realm of reason, so the police were obliged to investigate. The Chicago connection didn't pan out, so they took a closer look at the widow.

Hazel maintained that she and her niece Ethel had been in the living room of the home playing cards and listening to the radio, and they hadn't heard a thing. Ethel's version differed from her aunt's account—she said they'd heard the shot—but Hazel didn't give an inch under police questioning. In fact, she seemed to be taunting the investigators when she voluntarily allowed them to search the house. She told them they'd find guns, but none of

Opposite: Hazel Glab poses next to the bars in her cell at the Hall of Justice Jail in December 1935. She was facing trial for the murder of her husband eight years earlier. Prior to her arrest Hazel had granted Aggie Underwood an exclusive interview. To keep the other newshounds from stealing her thunder, Aggie took Hazel home with her. They arrived to find forty little girls from Aggie's daughter's Girl Scout troop enjoying a potluck dinner. Hazel pitched in and helped serve and then clean up. Unfortunately there is no merit badge for dining with a murderess.

them would be the murder weapon. The police searched the house and Hazel had told the truth. With no major leads forthcoming, the case went cold.

For the next few years all was quiet on the Hazel front; that is until 1935, when she was found guilty of forging the will of her deceased fiance, Albert Cheney. It was no wonder authorities were suspicious of the document. It had been written in long-hand in bright purple ink on hotel stationary. Of course Cheney had left everything to Hazel. Hazel was tried and convicted of forgery and sentenced to from one-and-a-half to nineteen years in prison.

Prior to her arrest, Hazel had granted Aggie Underwood an exclusive interview. To keep the other newshounds from stealing her thunder, Aggie took Hazel home with her. They arrived to find forty little girls from Aggie's daughter's Girl Scout troop enjoying a potluck dinner. Hazel pitched in and helped serve and then clean up.

The murder case against Hazel finally jelled when a woman came forward with information that finally led to an indictment. On March 30, 1936, Hazel was convicted of second degree murder and sentenced to from five years to life in the women's prison at Tehachapi.

Astonishingly, Hazel served the minimum of five years for John's murder and she was released in 1941. She had learned nothing from her time in prison and continued her life of crime until she passed away on September 9, 1977.

Opposite: A young and innocent-looking Hazel Belford (later Glab), as she appeared in 1916. She was cast in Thomas H. Ince's *The Deserter,* playing the role of Mary, for which she was credited. It is believed she was also cast in Thomas H. Ince's *Civilization* though she was probably an extra as she is not credited.

On April 2, 1936, Aggie Underwood accompanied Hazel Glab (holding magazine) and two other convicted murderesses on their trip from Los Angeles to the women's prison at Tehachapi. Once they had arrived at their destination, Hazel, still clutching the detective magazine she had brought with her, waved good-bye to Aggie and said, "Don't say I cried or carried on, because I'll be back."

Opposite: Photograph article dated June 20, 1928 reads, "Mrs. Hazel Glab, at right, testified today at the inquest into the death of her husband, John I. Glab, and composedly denied that she shot him. At left is her seventeen-year-old niece, Ethyl Kaser, who also is being held and questioned."

Never one to stay out of trouble permanently, Glab, now going by Hazel Stoddard was taken to court for allegedly making threats towards Mrs. Ione Selma (*left*) in 1965.

Opposite: Hazel was back in the news in April of 1958 when she was arrested for pandering, accused of offering a 27-year-old woman for prostitution.

The First with the Latest!

Hazel Glab

THELMA TODD

On Monday, December 16, 1935, the body of screen star Thelma Todd was discovered slumped over in the front seat of her twelve-cylinder, chocolate-brown Lincoln Phaeton. Thelma's maid, Mae Whitehead, had gone to the garage as she did every morning, to drive the big car down the hill for her employer's use. When she saw Thelma behind the wheel she thought that she was asleep—but on closer inspection, she realized that Thelma was dead. Mae immediately telephoned Roland West, Thelma's lover and partner in Thelma Todd's Sidewalk Café, above which Thelma had an apartment.

Roland telephoned the police and the investigation into the star's death began. From the moment the story broke, the local newspaper covered it as if there was something sinister about the circumstances. The *Record* proclaimed: "Thelma Todd Found Dead, Investigating Possible Murder." The *Herald* suggested her death was worthy of Edgar Allan Poe: "...if her death was accidental it was as strange an accident as was ever conceived by the brain of Poe." But was it?

At the autopsy, which Aggie Underwood attended, it was determined that Thelma's death had been the result of carbon monoxide poisoning. The twelve-cylinder car would have filled the closed garage with deadly gas in a matter of minutes. Despite an inquest which ruled the death an accident, there were suggestions of foul play.

Opposite: A picture of Thelma Todd taken in court at the time of her divorce from Pasquale J. De Cicco in 1934.

Captain Bert Wallis of the police homicide squad makes a check of the position of Thelma Todd's body where it was found in her car. The coroner's report said her death was caused by carbon monoxide poisoning, but doubt remained whether it was suicide, foul play or an accident. Thelma's autopsy was the first Aggie Underwood ever attended.

The First with the Latest!

Thelma's café was a roaring success and rumors had it that the east coast mobster, Lucky Luciano, had his eye on it as the possible site for illegal gambling—but Thelma wouldn't go for it. Did Luciano have Thelma murdered to get her out of the way?

What about Roland West? He had a tendency to be controlling and jealous. Thelma had attended a party at the Trocodero the night before her death. Had she arrived home much later than Roland had demanded? Did he discover her asleep in her car and close the garage doors? Perhaps he'd closed the doors to make her sick, not realizing how quickly the gas would kill her.

Aggie worked alongside a detective who was trying to tie up the loose ends. One night he received a call at his home warning him to "lay off if you know what is good for you." Who had threatened him? Neither he nor Aggie ever found out.

Thelma Todd's death remains one of Hollywood's most enduring mysteries.

Roland West, "best friend" and business partner of Thelma Todd, and ZaSu Pitts, film star and comedienne, talk in the corridor at the grand jury probe into Thelma's mysterious death. Both had been called to testify.

The First with the Latest!

This three-story, 15,000-square-foot Spanish style building housed Thelma Todd's Sidewalk Café and is still located at 17575 Pacific Coast Highway in Pacific Palisades. The *Herald Express* added labels to this picture of the area where Thelma Todd lived and died. The 270 steps are the ones she supposedly walked up to get to the garage where she died.

THE 270 STEPS.

THELMA TODD'S APARTMENT.

LOCATION OF HOUSE

THE JOYA CAFE.

SIDEWALK CAFE.

People from many walks of life, from children to the aged, rich and poor, came to the Pierce Brothers Mortuary, at 720 W. Washington Boulevard in the University Park neighborhood of Los Angeles, to view the body of the Thelma Todd which was on view from 8:00 a.m. to 1:00 p.m. on December 19, 1935. Police were called in for security because of the size of the crowd, but were not needed.

The First with the Latest!

Police stand outside the doorway of the Pacific Palisades garage where the body of Thelma Todd was found December 16, 1935. The garage of Castillo del Mar belonged to the beach home of Roland West, her business partner and manager of her seaside cafe. The newspaper wrote the words "What happened behind these doors?" across the picture for effect.

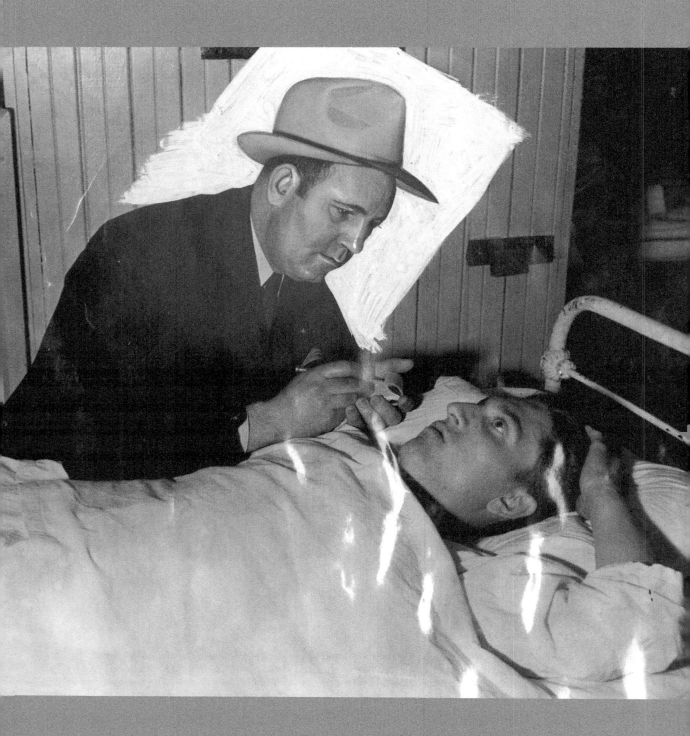

SAMUEL WHITTAKER

Retired church organist Samuel Whittaker and his wife, Ethel, had gone out on the evening of March 16, 1936. Shortly after their arrival home early the next morning, neighbors heard several gun shots. One of the neighbors, Henry Failer, came out of his apartment and saw a man leaving the Whittaker place. The young man ran up the stairs to the roof of the building while Failer entered the Whittaker apartment to see what was going on. He found Samuel holding a revolver in his right hand. Ethel was dead on the floor.

When the police arrived, Samuel told them that he and Ethel had been ambushed in their apartment that morning. A masked man stepped out of a closet and trained a gun on them. He demanded money, but then shot Ethel anyway. Samuel produced his own weapon and fired five shots, wounding but not killing the intruder.

The cops found James Fagan Culver at the next-door rooming house suffering from multiple gunshot wounds. They busted him for robbery and murder.

For the first couple of days following the crime, Samuel was hailed as a hero. But James told a far different story. He said that earlier that year he had hitchhiked from Kentucky; that he had met Samuel in front of a café early

Opposite: **While suffering from bullet wounds, James Fagan Culver (aka Jack Lane) is interrogated by Detective Lieutenant Warren Hudson in the murder of Ethel Whittaker. Initially the prime suspect in the killing, a bizarre plot involving Samuel Whittaker, the husband of the victim, was soon uncovered.**

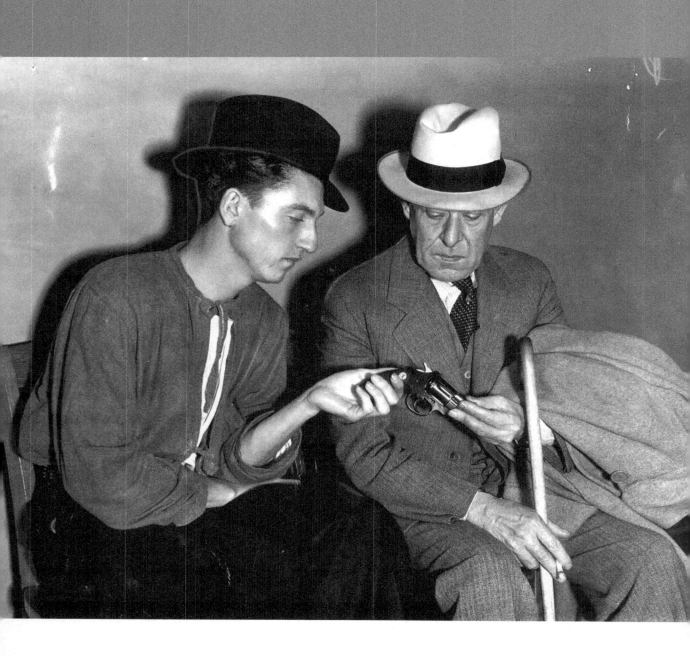

Samuel Whittaker (*left*) was a retired church organist and a man with a plan. He hired drifter James Culver (*right*) to fake a holdup. Ostensibly Whittaker wanted to teach his wife not to be careless with her jewelry. Whittaker's actual plan was to kill both his wife and Culver, and then blame the dead robber for everything. Whittaker was caught out by Aggie Underwood in March 1936 when she saw him wink conspiratorially at Culver during this photo shoot. She told LAPD detective Thad Brown what she'd seen and Whittaker was subsequently busted.

The First with the Latest!

one morning and asked him for money so he could eat. They struck up a conversation and then saw each other frequently. One day Samuel told James that he wanted to "thrill a lady friend" and stage a fake hold-up. Samuel gave James a gun and instructions to wait in a closet until he and his lady friend were in the room, fake the hold-up, and then flee.

Samuel had left out the salient features of his plan when he described it to James. What Samuel actually intended to do was to murder his wife, kill James, collect on an insurance policy, and walk away a hero. If he'd been a better shot, he may have gotten away with it.

Unfortunately for Samuel, Aggie was present at a photo shoot which had the two men facing each other. Aggie was stunned when she noticed Samuel deliberately wink at James. She drew LAPD detective Thad Brown aside and told him what she had witnessed. The detective uncovered the murder-for-hire plot and Samuel was convicted of killing his wife.

Samuel was quoted as saying that he hoped God would strike him dead if he was guilty of Ethel's slaying. As he was being booked into San Quentin, he dropped dead.

Samuel Whittaker (*right*) on the witness stand as James Fagan Culver (wearing mask) re-enacts the fake hold-up Whittaker had hired him to pull during the June 1936 trial.

The First with the Latest!

Samuel Whittaker on the witness stand holding the gun he used in the murder of his wife. When he was sentenced to life for his crime the pious church organist said that he hoped God would strike him dead if he was guilty. As he was being booked into San Quentin, he dropped dead.

Samuel Whittaker

Convicted killer Samuel Whittaker gets shackled by Deputy Sheriff E.H. Heddy on June 15, 1935 after being sentenced to life in prison at San Quentin. The stay would be a short one, as he dropped dead while being booked.

Opposite: Eulala Aston, sister of murder victim Ethel Whitaker reacts to her brother-in-law's guilty verdict. She was quoted as saying, "I'd rather have my murdered sister back again."

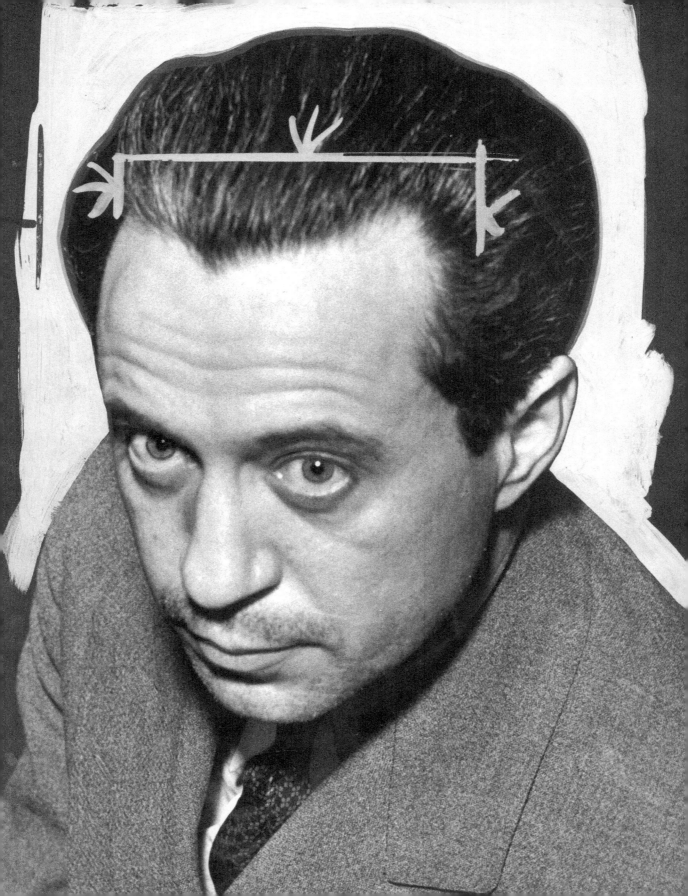

PAUL WRIGHT

P aul Wright, an aviation company executive, and his friend, John Kimmel, attended a private club meeting on the evening of November 9, 1937. After the meeting they went out for a nightcap at Clara Bow's It Café. It was getting very late, so Paul suggested that John accompany him home, ostensibly to provide back-up when his wife Evelyn questioned him about where, and with whom, he had spent the evening.

It was after 2 a.m. when they pulled up to Paul's hilltop home in Glendale. Once inside, Paul said he felt fatigued and went to the bedroom for a nap—leaving Evelyn to entertain John.

Paul later recalled the events of that night: "I was awakened by some sort of sound—like a piano. It startled me out of my sleep. I went to the living room door and saw that the lights were still on. Johnny was sitting at the piano. I could just see his head. He was looking downward. I couldn't see Evelyn and I wondered where she was."

It didn't take him long to figure out where his wife was. At that moment everything inside of Paul exploded in what he later described as a "white flame." He got his gun and shot John and Evelyn to death.

Paul was put on trial for the slayings. His attorney, Jerry Giesler, had conceived of a creative defense for his client. He said that Paul's WWI service (during which he was gassed), a post-war tuberculosis attack, and a

Opposite: Paul Wright (pictured) was found guilty of the murders of his wife and best friend. During the sanity hearing the jury found that while Wright had been insane at the time of killings, he had since regained his senses. He walked out of the courtroom a free man.

Paul Wright told cops that he had been sleeping when he heard the jangle of piano keys coming from his living room. He went to investigate and found his friend, John Kimmel, sitting on the piano bench and his wife, Evelyn, on her knees in front of him—and she wasn't tying his shoes. He seized his .38 and shot them both dead. Wright said he had been consumed by a white flame of passion.

The First with the Latest!

voluntary vasectomy combined to make him emotionally unstable—capable of more violent reactions to shock than normal men.

At the time of his arrest, Paul had confessed to the murders, but when he got to trial his story changed and his memory conveniently began to fail him. How would the jury view his shifting story?

The jury of eight men and four women listened to the X-rated testimony and contemplated Giesler's vasectomy defense. In the end they found Paul Wright guilty on two counts of manslaughter. But there was a twist—the jury also found that he had been insane at the time of the murders, so he was not guilty.

When the Lunacy Commission examined Wright, they concurred with the jury that Paul Wright was no longer insane. He was freed and would never serve a single day in prison.

Aggie Underwood, who covered the story, later referred to the Paul Wright trial as one in which "many observers believe that it showed Jerry Giesler at his greatest as a criminal lawyer."

Pictured is the house at 1830 Verdugo Vista Drive in Glendale where Paul Wright shot and killed his wife and best friend after discovering them in a compromising position.

Accused murderer Paul Wright on the witness stand with attorney Jerry Geisler. Aggie Underwood, who covered the story, later referred to the Paul Wright trial as one in which, "many observers believe that it showed Jerry Giesler at his greatest as a criminal lawyer."

Opposite: Mrs. Maureen Kimmel, widow of the slain John Kimmel sits by the piano at their Burbank home. Given the circumstances of Kimmel's death, the piano was an odd choice for a photo op.

LAUREL CRAWFORD

It was barely dawn on December 12, 1939, when Aggie Underwood and photographer Paul Pangburn rolled up to the scene of a tragic auto accident on the road from Mt. Wilson. Five people had perished when the light sedan in which they were riding careened down the mountainside. The dead were: Elva Ruth Crawford and her three children ranging in age from eight to fifteen, and a boarder in the Crawford home, Ralph Barnett. The only survivor was the driver of the car, Laurel Crawford.

Laurel rested on a cot surrounded by Sheriff's deputies who refused to allow Aggie to interview him. Understandably, the deputies felt that the man had been through an ordeal which could only be exacerbated by questions from the press. Still, Aggie managed to make a deal with a deputy who talked with Laurel as Aggie listened in from an adjoining room. She had used this ploy before.

There were a few things about Laurel and his story that felt wrong to Aggie. Laurel claimed that he had lost control of the car and even though he exhorted his passengers to jump, he was the only one who had managed to escape. He said he had climbed down the 1,000-foot embankment a couple of times. He held his daughter, Helen, in his arms as she died. But Aggie doubted his veracity. Helen's body had been crushed and bloody, yet Laurel's clothing was clean.

Opposite: Laurel Crawford looking calm and clean despite being in a horrific automobile accident hours before that claimed the life of his wife and three children. His unruffled appearance was Aggie's first tip-off of foul play.

The First with the Latest!

When Lieutenants Garner Brown and Paul Mahoney of the Sheriff's Bureau of Investigation arrived, Brown asked Aggie for her take on the situation. She answered bluntly: "I think it smells. He's guilty as hell." A few of the deputies appeared shocked, but Brown listened to her reasoning. She told him that Laurel's leather jacket, khaki pants and shirt were far too clean if he had been up and down the mountain as he had said. His grief rang false to Aggie too. He made the tragedy revolve around him, repeating: "Why did this have to happen to me?" rather than questioning why it had happened to his family.

Lieutenant Brown agreed with Aggie's assessment and pursued an investigation. It was discovered that Laurel had purchased insurance policies on his wife and children, a few with double indemnity clauses. He stood to receive a large payout which he then intended to use to purchase a car dealership.

Laurel Crawford was sentenced to four consecutive life sentences (he wasn't indicted for Barnett's death).

Thirty-one years later, in May 1971, at age 73, Laurel died of injuries he sustained during a beating meted out by other prisoners at Folsom.

Opposite: **Laurel Crawford points down the slope of 1000 foot cliff over which his automobile plunged killing his entire family. Crawford claimed that he had leaped from the car at the last moment and was spared. When Aggie Underwood arrived she had a hunch that Crawford's display of grief was phony. Sheriff's investigator Lieutenant Garner Brown asked her for her opinion. Without hesitation she said, "I think it smells. He's guilty as hell." She was right.**

Members of the California Conservation Corps assist in retrieving the bodies of the Crawford family from the bottom of a canyon near Mt. Wilson.

The First with the Latest!

Laurel Crawford (*center*) undergoes rigorous questioning by Los Angeles Police Department psychiatrist **Dr. Paul De River** (*left*) and Los Angeles County Sheriff's homicide inspector **William Penprase** (*right*). Dr. De River declared Crawford was "money mad" and had murdered his family to collect over $30,000 in life insurance.

Laurel Crawford

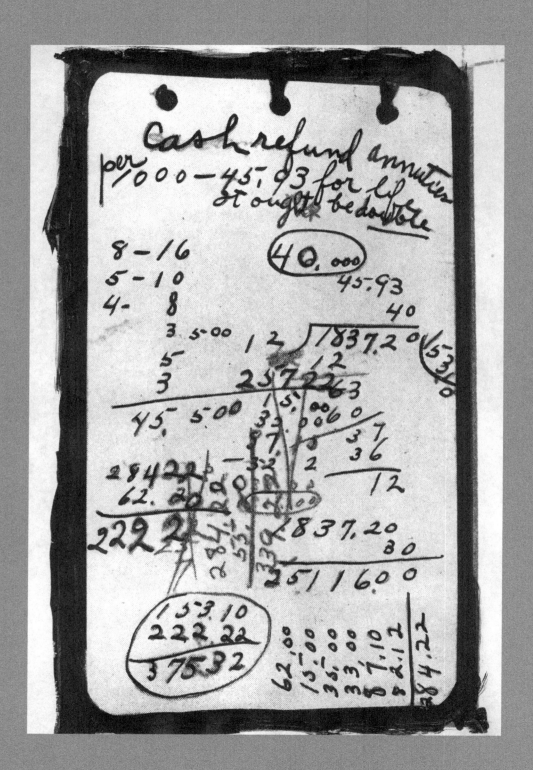

106 The First with the Latest!

Laurel Crawford enters the courthouse with his parents and foster sister, shortly before taking the stand in his murder trial. He maintained his innocence and wept openly on the stand while describing the accident which killed his wife, three kids, and a boarder.

Opposite: **One of the more damning pieces of evidence against Crawford was what the prosecution dubbed the "budget of death," with asserted calculations of an insurance payout.**

ERROL FLYNN

In 1942, swashbuckling actor and heartthrob, Errol Flynn, was accused of three felony counts of statutory rape involving two teenagers—Peggy Satterlee, fifteen, and Betty Hansen, seventeen. The trial took place during January and February of 1943, and if convicted, the star could have spent years in San Quentin.

Errol's first accuser, Peggy Satterlee, testified that she had been attacked by the actor while a guest on his ketch *Sirocco*. She and several other people were on a weekend cruise in the Santa Catalina Channel on August 2 and 3, 1941, when the alleged attack occurred. She told the jam-packed courtroom that she had been up on the deck as they approached Los Angeles Harbor when Errol joined her. She remarked on how pretty the moon looked and he allegedly told her: "It looks prettier through a porthole," as he escorted her to his stateroom.

One of the guests on the yacht, photographer Peter Stackpole, testified that Errol was holding one of the pictures of Peggy that had been taken over the weekend when he turned to Peter and said he was going to caption it "$5,000" because the girl was trying to shake him down.

Betty Hansen, Errol's second accuser, testified that the star had been intimate with her at the Bel-Air estate of Fred McEvoy, a British sportsman.

Neither girl's testimony withstood scrutiny. Peggy had given several conflicting statements before testifying in court. She had recently found a job

Opposite: **Errol Flynn signs an autograph for Pat Hovey who had hitchhiked from New Jersey to witness the actor's trial.**

The First with the Latest!

as a theater usherette, and on her application she gave her age as eighteen. When the theater manager questioned it, Peggy's mother declared: "My daughter *is* eighteen."

Betty Hansen's story didn't fare much better. While being held at Juvenile Hall, the young woman evidently told policewoman Mary Ross that it was "easy to get money in this sucker town." Ross also stated that Betty had told her she had undressed herself in the bedroom of the Bel-Air mansion—which didn't match her later statement that Errol had undressed her. The jury didn't find Peggy or Betty credible and acquitted Errol of all charges.

The trial proved to be a media frenzy, with throngs of fans showing up to get a look at their favorite movie star. Some had even made long trips from out of town to participate in the circus.

Aggie Underwood covered the entire trial. Following the acquittal, a party was held at Aggie Underwood's home. Errol supplied the liquor and Aggie cooked spaghetti for the celebrants.

Opposite: **Errol Flynn (*right center*) accompanied by his attorney, Jerry Giesler were surrounded by mostly female spectators as they entered the courtroom for Flynn's statutory rape trial. His two accusers had lied about everything, including their ages, and Flynn was acquitted. A post-trial party, which Flynn attended, was held at Aggie Underwood's home—she served spaghetti.**

Betty Hansen, 17, one of the two girls who charges film star Errol Flynn of attack, is shown at left, entering the courtroom for Flynn's trial. Many spectators, mostly women, anxiously try to enter.

The First with the Latest!

This was the dramatic scene in court when film star Errol Flynn rushed to the jury box to thank the jurors after he was acquitted of charges that he was intimate with two teenage girls. Smiling, the actor is shown shaking hands with jurors.

Errol Flynn faces a battery
of photographers after
denying charges that he
misconducted himself with
Peggy LaRue Satterlee
aboard his yacht during a
sailing trip to Catalina.

115

While his attorneys and the prosecution battle over the demands for a mistrial, Errol Flynn reads fan mail sent to him in care of the court.

The First with the Latest!

Peggy Satterle, testifying at the Flynn trial, smilingly refuses to look as Defense Attorney Jerry Giesler introduces into evidence a picture of herself wearing pigtails. The incident occurred after Giesler had questioned her regarding her age.

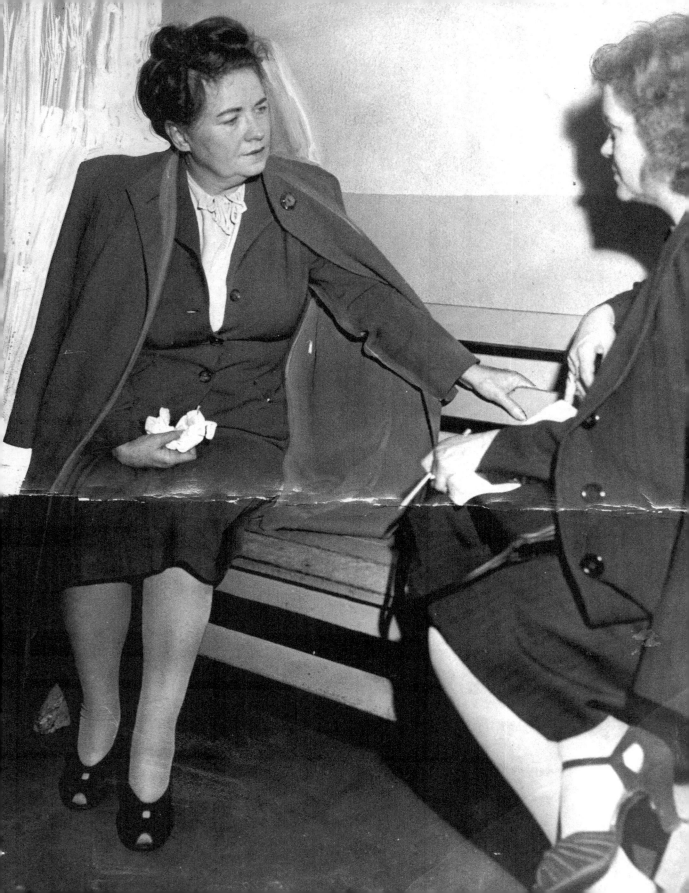

LOUISE PEETE

By the time she was in her late thirties, Louise Peete had left a trail of shattered lives in her wake from Boston, Massachusetts to Waco, Texas. She was the reason that two men had committed suicide; and she'd killed a man during an attempted rape—at least that was her story—the truth remains elusive.

In 1920, Louise relocated to Los Angeles where she met middle-aged mining executive Jacob Denton. Jacob was a recent widower, having lost both his wife and child in the Spanish Flu pandemic. Louise sized Jacob up as a man who would be susceptible to her Southern charm. When her attempts to get him to marry her failed, she ordered Jacob's caretaker to dump a ton of soil in the basement of the home. She said she intended to grow Jacob's favorite mushrooms there. But then on May 30, 1920, Jacob vanished.

For months, nobody questioned the tall tales Louise told to explain Jacob's disappearance, until his attorney finally contacted the police and asked them to search the house. It took the cops about an hour of digging to unearth Jacob's body. He had a bullet hole in his head.

On February 8, 1921, Louise was convicted of Jacob's murder and sentenced to life in prison. She served eighteen years before being paroled in for good behavior in 1939. Her incarceration had done nothing to change

Opposite: Louise Peete (*left*) interviewed by Aggie Underwood (*right*) for the last time in December of 1944. Louise was sentenced to death in the gas chamber for murder. When the death sentence was handed down Louise turned to Aggie, pinched her under the chin, and said, "Now don't you cry."

Louise Peete calmly takes the stand next to Judge Frank R. Willis during her 1921 murder trial. She was found guilty of shooting mining executive Jacob Denton and burying the body in the basement of his own home.

The First with the Latest!

her. She was out of prison for only five years before she killed again.

Louise's final victim was Margaret Logan, a Good Samaritan who offered the ex-con employment as a housekeeper and companion. Margaret's body was discovered in a shallow backyard grave at her Pacific Palisades home. An autopsy concluded that Margaret's death had been caused by a gunshot and a brutal beating.

Louise's protestations of outraged innocence fell on deaf ears and she was convicted of murder again. Only this time around, she was sentenced to death in the gas chamber. When the death sentence was handed down, Louise turned to Aggie, who had been reporting the entire case, pinched her under the chin, and said, "Now don't you cry."

A crowd of reporters spent time with Louise on her last night—among them was Aggie Underwood. Always a gracious hostess, Louise proffered a box of chocolates to be shared among them. Aggie later said of Louise: "She wasn't an artless little gun moll."

Lofie Louise Preslar Peete was executed on April 11, 1947. She was only the second woman to die in California's gas chamber; two others would follow her.

Standing in between Public Defenders Ellery Cuff (*left*), and William B. Neely, Louise Peete displays no emotion in 1945 while receiving a death sentence in the San Quentin gas chamber.

9-15-A.M. —   San Quentin California
                     April 11-1947
Rear Mr Barnard.
                My train is due at 10 A.M. —
I waited until the last moment before send-
ing you a special message. I am
sure you know what it is. — As one
with ability to see "the news behind the news"
you know it adds up to high esteem and
trust and deep abiding gratitude for every
thing. — If I am able to read newspapers it
shall be something you will —
          Sincerely
                Louise Peete.

9-2 7½ A.M. —

The press gathered at San Quentin on April 11, 1947 for Louise Peete's execution. Louise had left a trail of misery in her wake for decades. Despite her crimes, the killer was a gracious hostess. She passed around a box of chocolates for the reporters to enjoy before she was taken to the gas chamber. Would you accept candy from a multiple murderer?

Opposite: Mere hours before making her way to the San Quentin gas chamber, Louise Peete wrote three letters, one of which was to *Los Angeles Herald* reporter Barney Barnard in which she noted "my train is due at 10am," and that she held Barnard in high esteem for his ability to see "the news behind the news." By this time, Aggie had been made City Editor, but still attended the execution.

Louise Peete

LOIS AND LEON BENON

Navigating married life can be tough for adults, but when teenagers enter into matrimony it can be murder.

Leon (17) and Lois Benon (16) marked their first wedding anniversary on July 26, 1945, by having dinner at home with another couple, thirty-one-year-old Harold Young and his wife Zelpha. During the course of the get-together Harold, whose real name was William Douglas "Dee" Owens, persuaded Lois to run off to Texas with him.

Owens was the father of a five-year-old, but having a family had done nothing to cool his ardor for Lois. He had been pursuing the newlywed for months and had finally succeeded in winning her over with promises of a convertible coupe and "all the clothes she wanted."

Lois waited until everyone had finished their dinner, and then told Leon that she was running away with Dee. She went into the bedroom and began to pack her bag. Leon seemed to have taken the dissolution of his marriage in stride. He told Lois that if she wanted to leave, it was okay with him, "if that's the way you want it."

But losing Lois wasn't okay with Leon no matter what he'd said. He went to a bureau drawer and got out his disassembled .22 automatic rifle and began putting it together. Suddenly he had Lois's full attention. "What

Opposite: Leon Benon (*left*) comforts his wife Lois. The teenagers had been married for only one year when Lois declared that she was going to run off with William Owens. William, twelve years her senior, with a wife and three kids, had promised to buy the girl a convertible and all the clothes she wanted. Leon put an end to the plan when he shot William to death with a .22 caliber rifle.

Zelpha Owens, widow of the murder victim and eyewitness Frances Smith share a light moment during Leon Benon's trial.

are you going to do?" Leon loaded the weapon and told her he was going to go into the backyard and practice shooting. Dee saw what was happening and tried to get the gun away from Leon, but he wouldn't give it up.

Just as Lois and Dee were about to leave, Leon announced: "Well, Dee, you asked for it," and started firing. He didn't stop until his rival hit the floor. The police were called and Leon admitted to them that he had known about Lois and Dee for two months, and it was then that he had made up his mind to kill Dee.

While the underage Lois was being held at Juvenile Hall, Aggie Underwood took the opportunity to interview her. She later recalled, "While thoughts of homicide were as far from me when I was her age as I hoped it always would be, I believe I know how to talk to a girl of sixteen. As I primed the interview with sympathetic questions, the kid broke down and cried, and the photog captured the drama in his shots."

Leon, still a juvenile, was to be tried as an adult. His future looked grim. His defense was that he had been defending the sanctity of his home. The jury of eleven women and one man deliberated for more than 24 hours before acquitting the teenager.

Did the Benon's marriage survive? Of course not—on August 9, 1946, Leon was granted an annulment.

Opposite: A distraught Lois Benton leaves the courthouse with an unidentified woman. When Aggie first interviewed Lois she, "primed the interview with sympathetic questions, the kid broke down and cried."

Zelpha Owens (*left*), widow of Lois Benon's dead lover, looks more bemused than angry as she stops to stare at Leon and Lois Benon as they consult with their attorney.

***Opposite*: Leon Benton recounts the slaying of William Douglas Owens during his murder trial.**

The First with the Latest!

ARTHUR EGGERS

Fifty-two-year-old Arthur Eggers was a sworn Deputy Sheriff working as a desk clerk in the Temple City Substation. Arthur seemed to everyone to be a meek little man who possessed an inordinate amount of patience, who was intimidated by his own shadow, and dominated by his wife.

Over the years, his wife Dorothy had taunted her mild-mannered husband with ribald tales of hitch-hiking and picking up truckers. How often had he visualized Dorothy at a truck stop in the arms of a sweaty antithesis of himself? It would have been enough to drive any man completely mad. Neighbors of the Eggers' recalled that Dorothy had an unseemly number of male callers and rumors of Dorothy's infidelities had been reaching Arthur's ears for a very long time before he finally snapped under their weight.

In fact, it was the sighting of one of Dorothy's male "friends" that ultimately pushed Arthur over the edge into murder. He'd arrived home from work about 1 a.m. on December 28, 1946, to see the dark figure of a man exiting the back door of his home.

Once inside the house, Arthur confronted a completely naked Dorothy with what he'd seen and accused her of having an affair. Rather than being contrite, or even denying everything, Arthur later claimed that Dorothy laughed at him and said that if she was having an affair, what was he going to do about it?

Opposite: Former Sheriff's Deputy Arthur Eggers holds his head in anguish as he undergoes rigorous questioning about the murder of his wife, Dorothy.

Arthur Eggers raised his right hand and swore to Aggie Underwood that he could not possibly have murdered his wife, Dorothy, or cut of her head and hands because, "As God is my judge, we had rabbits once and I couldn't even butcher them."

The First with the Latest!

Paul Mahoney with the Sheriff's Office studies bloodstains on the bathroom floor of Arthur Eggers house where his wife Dorothy was suspected of being killed.

What he did about it was grab a gun, pump a couple of rounds into her and then, in a blind rage years in the making, cut off her head and hands. He wrapped his dead wife in a blanket and drove out to the Rim of the World Highway where he dumped her body. Somewhere along the way he had discarded her head and hands—they were never found.

He filed a missing persons report on Dorothy, but his co-workers became suspicious of him and an investigation was launched. A headless, handless body was discovered within hours after it had been dumped, and was subsequently identified as Dorothy because of surgery she'd had to remove bunions on her feet.

In an exclusive jail house interview, Arthur swore to Aggie Underwood that he was too chicken-hearted to commit murder: "I couldn't even kill a rabbit." he said.

Arthur may not have been a rabbit killer, but he was found to be a wife slayer and sentenced to death. He was executed in the gas chamber at San Quentin.

Aggie Underwood (*foreground*) waits to interview suspected wife slayer, Arthur Eggers (handcuffed).

Opposite: Pictured are the gun and saw Arthur Eggers used in the murder and dismemberment of his wife, Dorothy. Her body was discovered along a mountain road, but the head and hands remain missing.

ELIZABETH SHORT *AKA* BLACK DAHLIA

On the morning of January 15, 1947, Los Angeles was in the grip of a cold wave with temperatures dropping below freezing. Mrs. Betty Bersinger was walking south on Norton with her three-year-old daughter Anne. Bersinger noticed something pale in weeds about a foot in from the sidewalk; it was the nude body of a young woman. At first Bersinger thought it was a mannequin or, if a real woman, perhaps she was drunk. But that was before she saw that the body had been cut in half. Bersinger said "I was terribly shocked and scared to death, I grabbed Anne and we walked as fast as we could to the first house that had a telephone."

Officers and detectives from the Los Angeles Police Department arrived and so did dozens of newspaper reporters—among them was Aggie Underwood. There was nothing at the scene which could be used to identify the dead woman. They rolled her prints at the morgue but couldn't send them to the FBI in Washington, D.C. because severe winter storms were grounding planes.

Warden Woolard, Assistant Managing Editor of the *Herald*, had a brainstorm about Jane Doe's fingerprints. The paper had recently purchased some fairly new technology—a Soundphoto machine—that Woolard thought might be used to transmit the victim's prints to the FBI. Woolard spoke with LAPD Captain Jack Donahoe about the idea and both agreed that it was worth a shot. The dead girl was identified as twenty-two-year-old Elizabeth

Opposite: **One of the few photos the *Herald Express* obtained of Elizabeth Short before her gruesome slaying.**

Short. The *Herald* had scored a major scoop and the cops had identified the victim.

Two seasoned LAPD detectives, Harry Hansen and Finis Brown, were put in charge of the investigation. During the first twenty-four hours officers pulled in over 150 men for questioning. It was the largest manhunt since the 1927 kidnapping and murder of a twelve-year-old school girl, Marion Parker. Street cops knocked on hundreds of doors looking for a crime scene, but they never found the place where Elizabeth had been murdered.

When Elizabeth's Long Beach friends were questioned, they mentioned that they had nicknamed her the Black Dahlia. The name came from the fact that Elizabeth usually wore black, and from a movie they had seen together during the summer of 1946, *The Blue Dahlia*.

On Friday, January 17, 1947, a photograph of Elizabeth appeared on the front page of the *Herald-Express*, and the caption read "The Black Dahlia." She would never be called anything else.

Aggie interviewed Robert "Red" Manley, the first serious suspect in the Black Dahlia case, and she was prepared to follow the story to its conclusion when, without warning, she was pulled off of it and ultimately promoted to City Editor.

Aggie never understood the timing of her promotion—she would have preferred to follow the Dahlia story until it went cold. But it was an important moment in her career and for women in journalism—Aggie was the first woman in the U.S. to become the City Editor of a major metropolitan newspaper.

Decades have passed without a solution to Elizabeth's murder. It is still city's most famous unsolved homicide case.

Opposite: **Robert Manley's portrait looks like a still from a film noir. He was the first suspect in the slaying of Elizabeth Short, aka the Black Dahlia. Aggie Underwood interviewed Manley and concluded that he was innocent—the cops agreed and released him. The infamous unsolved murder was the last case that Aggie covered as a reporter. A few weeks into the case she was promoted to city editor of the *Herald*.**

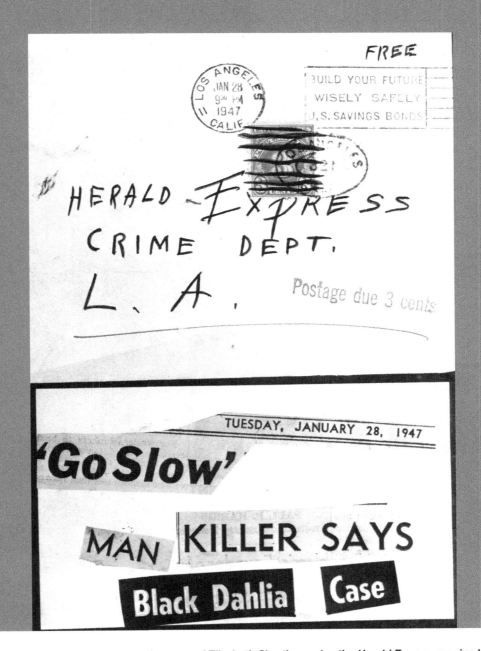

In the weeks following the discovery of Elizabeth Short's murder, the *Herald Express* received numerous letters and notes purporting to give information to help solve the case which still remains unsolved.

Opposite: Pictured here on the telephone is Betty Bersinger, the woman who was walking by a vacant lot with her young daughter and discovered Elizabeth Short's body.

Phoebe Short and Mrs. Virginia West, mother and sister of victim Elizabeth Short are seated in the homicide investigation room of the police station. Next to Mrs. West is her husband Adrian. The two men on the left in the picture are Coroner Ben Brown and Chief Deputy Coroner Victor Wallage.

The First with the Latest!

ABOUT THE AUTHOR

Joan Renner is a writer, social historian, and lecturer. Her blog, *Deranged L.A. Crimes*®, recounts true tales of murder, mayhem, political corruption, and celebrity scandal from the 1920s through the 1970s.

Joan has appeared in numerous episodes of *Deadly Affairs, Evil Twins, Deadly Women, Evil Kin,* and *Dark Temptations* for the ID Discovery Channel. She appeared in a segment on film noir for the Turner Classic Movies series *Film Fanatics,* and in an episode about 1930s era gangsters for the History Channel.

As a volunteer for the Los Angeles Police Museum, Joan has assisted with archival projects, research, and exhibits. In spring 2015, she completed a book with the museum entitled *LAPD '53.* Co-authored by novelist James Ellroy and the museum's executive director, Glynn Martin, the book spent four weeks on the *Los Angeles Times* Bestseller List.

Joan's true crime book, *Deranged L.A. Crimes from the Notebook of Aggie Underwood* will be released in Fall 2015.

Opposite: **Aggie hard at work on the City Desk in 1961.**

ABOUT THE PHOTO COLLECTION

The Los Angeles Public Library (LAPL) began collecting photographs sometime before World War II and had a collection of about 13,000 images by the late 1950s. In 1981, when Los Angeles celebrated its 200th birthday, Security Pacific National Bank gave its noted collection of historical photographs to the people of Los Angeles to be archived at the Central Library. Since then, LAPL has been fortunate to receive other major collections, making the Library a resource worldwide for visual images.

Notable collections include the "photo morgues" of the *Los Angeles Herald Examiner* and *Valley Times* newspapers, the Kelly-Holiday mid-Century collection of aerial photographs, the Works Progress Administration/Federal Writers Project collection, the Luther Ingersoll Portrait Collection, along with the landmark *Shades of L.A.*, which is an archive of images representing the contemporary and historic diversity of families in Los Angeles. Images were chosen from family albums and copied in a project sponsored by Photo Friends.

The Los Angeles Public Library Photo Collection also includes the works of individual photographers, including Ansel Adams, Herman Schultheis, William Reagh, Ralph Morris, Lucille Stewart, Gary Leonard, Stone Ishimaru, Carol Westwood, and Rolland Curtis.

Over 100,000 images from these collections have been digitized and are available to view through the LAPL website at **http://photos.lapl.org.**

ABOUT PHOTO FRIENDS

Formed in 1990, Photo Friends is a nonprofit organization that supports the Los Angeles Public Library's Photograph Collection and History & Genealogy Department. Our goal is to improve access to the collections and promote them through programs, projects, exhibits, and books such as this one.

We are an enthusiastic group of photographers, writers, historians, business people, politicians, academics, and many others—all bonded by our passion for photography, history, and Los Angeles.

Since 1994, Photo Friends has presented a series called *The Photographer's Eye*, which spotlights local photographers and their work. These talks are presented bi-monthly. In 2011, Photo Friends inaugurated *L.A. in Focus*, a lecture series that features images drawn primarily from the Photo Collection. We have presented programs on L.A. crime, the San Fernando Valley, Kelly-Holiday aerial photographs, and L.A.'s themed environments, among others.

With initial funding from the Ralph M. Parsons Foundation, Photo Friends sponsored *L.A. Neighborhoods Project* by commissioning photographers to create a visual record of the neighborhoods of Los Angeles during the early part of the 21st century (all now part of the collection). To ensure the Library's Collection will continue to reflect such an important part of Los Angeles's history, a generous grant enabled Photo Friends to hire five contemporary photographers to document present-day industrial L.A. These images have become part of LAPL's permanent collection and are available through the Library's Photo Database. Photo Friends also curates photography exhibits on display in the History Department.

Photo Friends is a membership organization. Please consider becoming a member and helping us in our work to preserve and promote L.A.'s rich photographic resource. All proceeds from the sale of this book go to support Photo Friends' programs.

photofriends.org